BEANO

FIVE a DAY

JOKE
BOOK

A STUDIO PRESS BOOK

First published in the UK in 2021 by Studio Press Books,
an imprint of Bonnier Books UK,
4th Floor, Victoria House, Bloomsbury Square, London WC1B 4DA
Owned by Bonnier Books,
Sveavägen 56, Stockholm, Sweden

bonnierbooks.co.uk
beano.com

1 3 5 7 9 10 8 6 4 2

ISBN 978-1-80078-117-7

Edited by Ellie Rose
Designed by Deryck Tilling and Rob Ward
Production by Emma Kidd

A CIP catalogue for this book is available from the British Library
Printed and bound in the UK

BEANO®
FIVE a DAY
JOKE BOOK

CONTENTS

Five laughs a day are proven to be good for you and this book is your prescription for big lolz!

The *Beano* Boffins have been hard at work selecting the very best rib-busting jokes just for you. Each joke has passed the chuckle test so all you have to do is pick five fab funnies every single day!

And, as laughter is the best medicine, don't forget to share the fun with your friends and family. Turn to page eight for some top joke-telling tips to help you.

BEANO
BRITAIN'S FUNNIEST CLASS

Get ready, get set, get joking!

Here at *Beano* HQ we've been searching up and down the nation to find **Britain's Funniest Class**.

We've had hundreds of entries to the competition and have been laughing non-stop at your gags. It's been a tough decision but we finally managed to narrow it down to a shortlist of ten top-class jokes.

So, drumroll please... turn to page 108 to read the gag crowned champion and the worthy runners-up!

TOP TIPS FOR GUARANTEED GIGGLES

Telling a joke is about more than just saying it out loud. If you want to be truly funny, follow our top-secret formula that will even have your teachers rolling around laughing.

THE FUNNY FORMULA

RELAX.

Smile. Imagine your best friend just sat on a whoopee cushion. If you're in a good mood, your audience will be too. They'll be ready to laugh!

GIVE IT OOMPH.

Make sure that your voice goes up and down as you speak to bring your joke to life. Add a pinch of pizzazz! A sprinkling of zing! The last thing you want to do is sound as if you're reading the newzzzzzz…

STOP.

Before you deliver the punchline – the funny bit at the end of the joke – pause for a second. Then your audience will be on the edge of their seats, wondering what you're going to say next. It'll make them *even more ready* to laugh.

WAIT.

Yayyyyyy. You're a comedy genius! You've delivered the punchline and your audience is rolling in the aisles! They're clutching their sides! They're crying with laughter! And here's the important part: pause before rushing onto your next joke. Give the crowd a chance to laugh. If you tell another joke now, they won't hear you. Besides, laughing is FUN. So let them guffaw and giggle and chortle and chuckle for a few seconds before blasting them with your next comedy masterpiece.

RELAX + GIVE IT OOMPH + STOP + WAIT = MEGALOLZ

SCHOOL

Why did the mushroom hate going to school?

Because he was always spored!

Why did the school ban scissors?

To stop people cutting class!

Why did the robot go back to school?

Her skills were a little rusty!

Why did the boy eat his homework?

Because his teacher said it was a piece of cake!

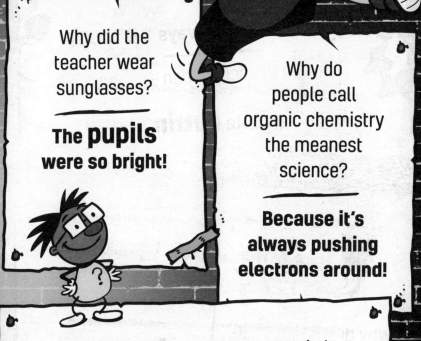

Why did the teacher wear sunglasses?

The **pupils** were so bright!

Why do people call organic chemistry the meanest science?

Because it's always pushing electrons around!

Teacher: Didn't I tell you to stand at the back of the queue?

Student: I tried but there was someone already there!

SCHOOL

WHAT DO YOU LEARN
AT WITCH SCHOOL?

SPELLING!

WHY COULDN'T THE MATHS STUDENT
GET ANY ATTENTION?

HE DIDN'T **COUNT!**

WHY DIDN'T RUDOLPH GO TO SCHOOL?

HE WAS **ELF-**TAUGHT!

WHERE DO KITTENS GO ON
SCHOOL TRIPS?

THE **MEW**SEUM!

WHY DID THE MUSIC TEACHER NEED A LADDER?

TO REACH THE **HIGH** NOTES!

WHAT HAPPENS TO WITCHES WHO BREAK THE SCHOOL RULES?

THEY GET EX**SPELLED**!

WHY DID THE ZOMBIE STAY HOME FROM SCHOOL?

HE FELT **ROTTEN**!

SCHOOL

WHAT DO ELVES LEARN IN SCHOOL?

THE **ELF**ABET!

WHY DID THE TEACHER GO
TO THE BEACH?

TO **TEST** THE WATER!

WHAT DO YOU GET IF YOU CROSS A
TEACHER WITH A VAMPIRE?

A **BLOOD** TEST!

WHY DID THE ECHO
GET DETENTION?

FOR **ANSWERING** BACK!

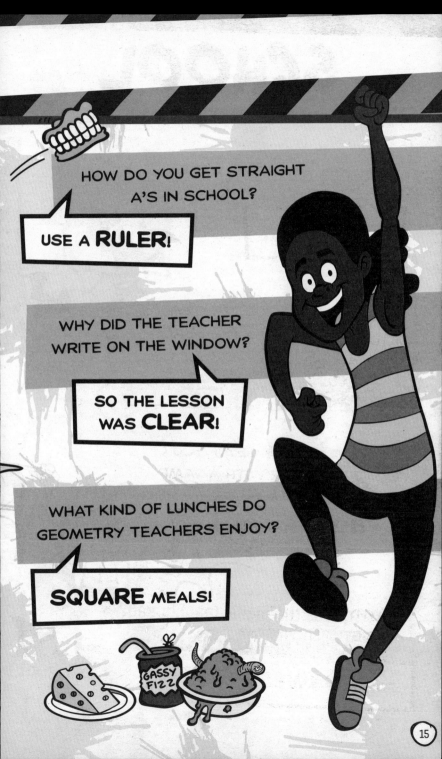

SCHOOL

What do you do
if your teacher rolls
their eyes at you?

Roll them back!

Why were the teacher's eyes crossed?

**Because she couldn't
control her pupils!**

What school teaches you to greet people?

High school!

Why was the music teacher sad?

He had lots of trebles!

Why is an English teacher like a judge?

They both hand out long sentences!

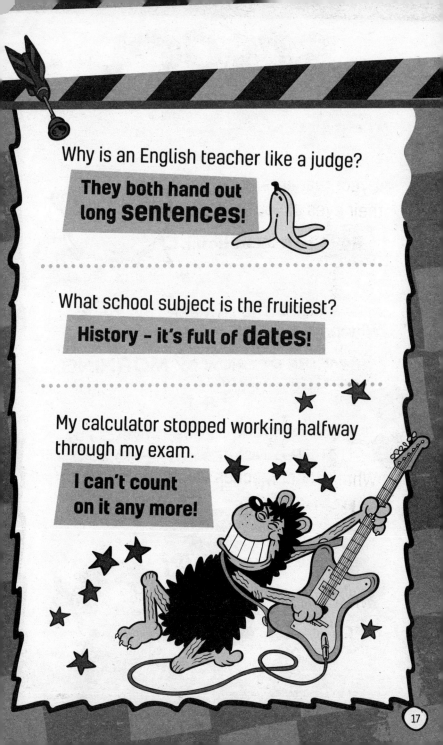

What school subject is the fruitiest?

History – it's full of dates!

My calculator stopped working halfway through my exam.

I can't count on it any more!

SCHOOL

MY PIRATE FRIEND JUST
GOT HIS EXAM RESULTS.

 ALL **HIGH C'S!**

WHAT'S THE NUMBER ONE THING
KIDS WISH FOR ON A SUNDAY NIGHT?

A METRE OF SNOW BY **MORNING!**

WHAT DO SCHOOL BUS DRIVERS PUT
ON THEIR PANCAKES IN THE MORNING?

TRAFFIC **JAM!**

MY FAVOURITE TEACHER
AT SCHOOL WAS MRS TURTLE.
SHE **TORTOISE** WELL!

★ ★ ★

I'M A BIG FAN OF WHITE BOARDS.
THEY'RE RE-**MARKABLE**!

★ ★ ★

WHAT IS A CAT'S FAVOURITE
SHAKESPEARE PLAY?
Ro**MEOW** AND **MEW**LIET!

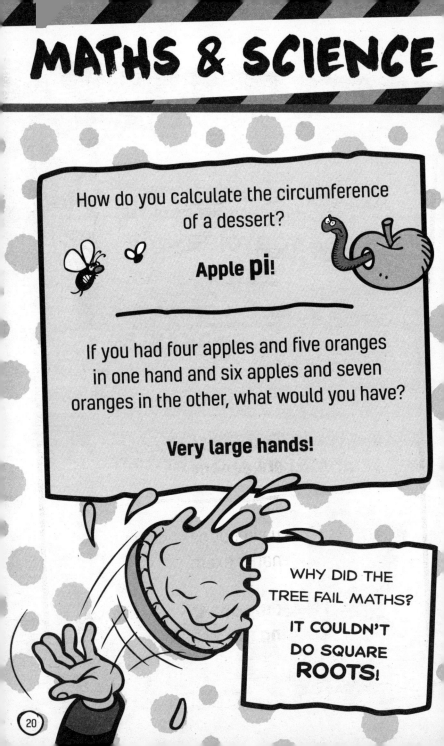

How do you calculate the circumference of a dessert?

Apple pi!

If you had four apples and five oranges in one hand and six apples and seven oranges in the other, what would you have?

Very large hands!

WHY DID THE TREE FAIL MATHS?

IT COULDN'T DO SQUARE **ROOTS!**

WHAT'S THE MOST MATHEMATICAL ASPECT OF SUMMER?

THE **TAN** LINES!

I failed my calculus test because I was seated between two identical twins.

I couldn't differentiate between them!

I'm nervous about passing my maths exam.

I think my chances of passing are 40-40!

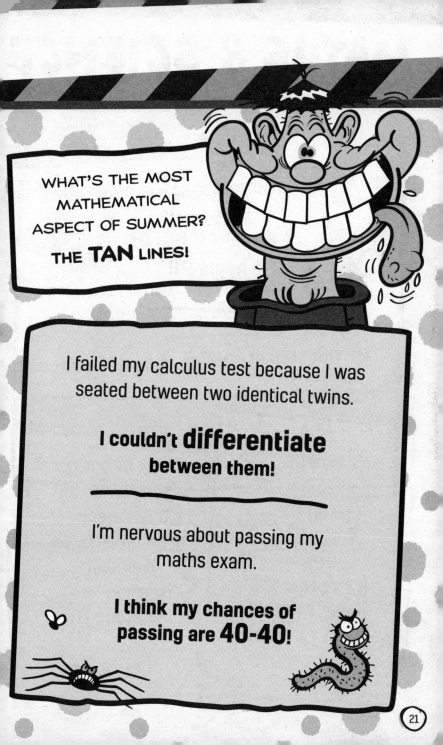

How does a mathematician plough his fields?

With a protractor!

Did you hear about the mathematician who's afraid of negative numbers?

He will stop at nothing to avoid them!

How do mathematicians tell off their children?

If I've told you once, I've told you n+1 times!

What do you get if you divide the circumference of a pumpkin by its diameter?

Pumpkin pi!

Teacher: If you got £20 from five people, what do you get?

Student: A new bike!

Did you hear about the constipated maths teacher?

He had to work it out with a pencil!

What kind of maths do owls like?

Owlgebra!

To the mathematicians who thought of the idea of zero…

Thanks for nothing!

WHY WAS THE MATHS STUDENT SO BAD AT DECIMALS?

SHE COULDN'T GET THE **POINT**!

WHY IS SIX AFRAID OF SEVEN?

BECAUSE SEVEN **ATE** NINE!

What do ducks use
in maths class?

A quackulator!

Why should you never do
maths in the jungle?

**Because if you add four
and four, you might get ate!**

Why was the maths book sad?

It had too many problems!

Why can't you make a crumble
with 3.14 apples?

Because that would be a pi!

Why did the scientist
go to the beach?

To test the water!

Scientists have discovered that
diarrhoea is hereditary...

It runs in your genes!

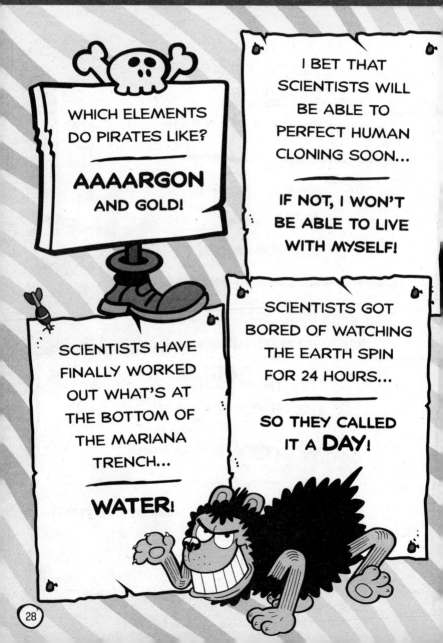

WHICH ELEMENTS DO PIRATES LIKE?

AAAARGON AND GOLD!

I BET THAT SCIENTISTS WILL BE ABLE TO PERFECT HUMAN CLONING SOON...

IF NOT, I WON'T BE ABLE TO LIVE WITH MYSELF!

SCIENTISTS HAVE FINALLY WORKED OUT WHAT'S AT THE BOTTOM OF THE MARIANA TRENCH...

WATER!

SCIENTISTS GOT BORED OF WATCHING THE EARTH SPIN FOR 24 HOURS...

SO THEY CALLED IT A **DAY!**

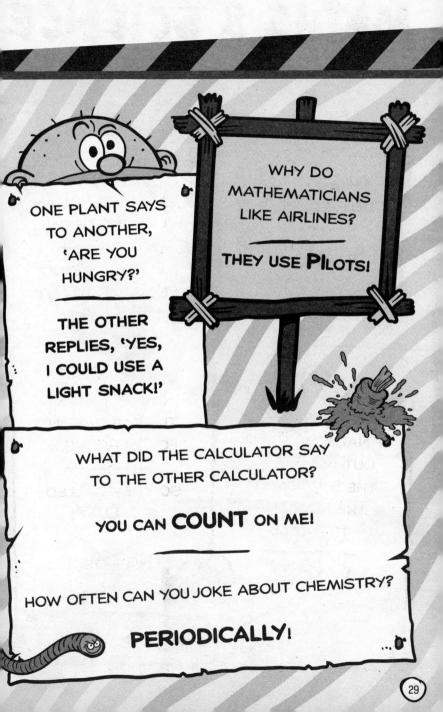

ONE PLANT SAYS TO ANOTHER, 'ARE YOU HUNGRY?'

THE OTHER REPLIES, 'YES, I COULD USE A LIGHT SNACK!'

WHY DO MATHEMATICIANS LIKE AIRLINES?

THEY USE **PI**LOTS!

WHAT DID THE CALCULATOR SAY TO THE OTHER CALCULATOR?

YOU CAN **COUNT** ON ME!

HOW OFTEN CAN YOU JOKE ABOUT CHEMISTRY?

PERIODICALLY!

MATHS & SCIENCE

WHAT IS HIJKLMNO?

H2O!

CARBON AND HYDROGEN WENT ON A DATE.

I HEARD THEY REALLY **BONDED!**

WHY CAN YOU NEVER TRUST ATOMS?

THEY MAKE UP **EVERYTHING!**

WHICH BODY PART IS THE NOISIEST?

THE EAR **DRUM!**

31

IDEA!

Why do people hate gravity?

It's always bringing them down!

Gravity is one of the most fundamental forces in the universe...

But if you remove it, you get gravy!

WINDY BEANS

WHAT IS ALBERT EINSTEIN'S RAPPER NAME?

MC **SQUARED!**

EINSTEIN DEVELOPED A THEORY ABOUT SPACE...

ABOUT **TIME**, TOO!

Which is faster, hot or cold?

Hot. You can always catch a cold!

What do physicists enjoy doing the most at sporting events?

The wave!

MATHS & SCIENCE

I'M READING A BOOK ABOUT ANTI-GRAVITY...

IT'S IMPOSSIBLE TO PUT **DOWN**!

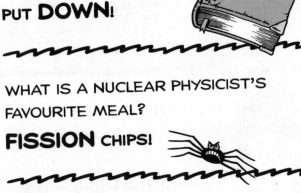

WHAT IS A NUCLEAR PHYSICIST'S FAVOURITE MEAL?

FISSION CHIPS!

WHERE DOES BAD LIGHT END UP?

IN A **PRISM**!

I'D TELL YOU A CHEMISTRY JOKE...

BUT I KNOW I WOULDN'T GET A **REACTION**!

WHY CAN'T YOU TAKE ELECTRICITY TO A PARTY?

BECAUSE IT DOESN'T KNOW HOW TO **CONDUCT** ITSELF!

WHAT DID ONE QUANTUM PHYSICIST SAY WHEN HE WANTED TO FIGHT ANOTHER QUANTUM PHYSICIST?

LET ME **ATOM**!

ENGLISH

I went to the library to get a medical book on abdominal pain.

Somebody had torn the appendix out!

★ ★ ★

Why did the teacher write on the window?

Because they wanted the lesson to be very clear!

★ ★ ★

I'm writing a book about the advantages and disadvantages of being an author and a scammer.

It's called prose and cons!

What did the sketchbook
say to the novel?

I'm drawing a blank!

★ ★ ★

I had plans to read a book about sinkholes...

But they fell through!

★ ★ ★

I just finished a book about Mount Everest...

It was a cliff hanger!

ENGLISH

WANT TO HEAR A JOKE ABOUT A PIECE OF PAPER?

NEVER MIND... IT'S **TEARABLE**!

WHY COULDN'T THE READING ADDICT STOP BUYING BOOKS?

THEY HAD NO **SHELF** CONTROL!

WHY DID THE ROMANIAN STOP READING AT NIGHT?

THEY WERE GIVING THE **BUCHAREST**!

A book fell on my head...

I only have mySHELF to blame!

What's a rabbit's favourite novel?

Warren Peace!

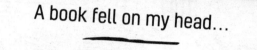

Why did the
children eat their
homework?

**Because the
teacher said
it was a piece
of cake!**

Is there a word that
contains all the
vowels including y?

Unquestionably!

What do you call Tom Sawyer's friend after he lost a lot of weight?

Huckleberry Thin!

Why are books always scared of their sequel?

Because they're after them!

I asked the librarian if I could have a burger and chips. They said, 'This is a library!'

So I whispered, 'Can I have a burger and chips?'

ENGLISH

I just read a book about helium.

I couldn't put it down!

Which books are hardest
to force yourself to read?

Friction books!

How many books can you
fit in an empty backpack?

One – after that it's not empty!

Who's a robot's favourite author?

Anne **Droid**!

Why should you not
write a book on penguins?

**Because writing a book
on paper is much easier!**

I went into a bookshop and asked if they
had any books about turtles. The cashier
asked, hardback?

I said, yeah, and little heads!

ENGLISH

WHO WRITES BOOKS FOR SMALL INSECTS?

BEETRIX POTTER!

I'VE GOT A BOOK IN MY BATHROOM THAT I WRITE MY FEELINGS AND PERSONAL THOUGHTS IN WHILE ON THE TOILET.

I CALL IT MY **DIARRHOEA**!

WHAT DOES A WASP SAY WHEN IT IS HAVING AN IDENTITY CRISIS?

TOO BEE OR NOT **TOO BEE**?

WHY DID THE LIBRARIAN GET KICKED OFF THE PLANE?

BECAUSE IT WAS **OVERBOOKED**!

ENGLISH

Which letter is small and green?

P!

What is the longest word?

Smiles – there's a mile between the first and last letters!

PHUT!

WHICH DINOSAUR KNEW THE MOST WORDS?

THE **THESAURUS**!

WHY ARE WRITERS ALWAYS COLD?

BECAUSE OF ALL THE **DRAFTS**!

Which building is the tallest?

The **library**... it has the most stories!

I saw someone spill letter tiles on the road...

I asked them what was the word on the street!

ENGLISH

Mum's spaghetti got in the Guinness Book of Records...

I hope she cleans the pages!

I finally found my book of maps...

Atlast!

What does a librarian take fishing?

Bookworms!

When is a green book not green?

When it's read!

Where do books like to sleep?

Under their covers!

I was reading some books about loud music...

 But there were too many volumes!

HISTORY & GEOGRAPHY

WHAT WAS THE ATMOSPHERE LIKE WHEN THE PAST, PRESENT AND FUTURE WALKED INTO CLASS?

TENSE!

WHAT MOUSE WAS A ROMAN EMPEROR?

JULIUS **CHEESER!**

HOW DID THE ROMANS CUT THEIR HAIR?

WITH A PAIR OF **CAESARS!**

A ROMAN WALKS INTO A CAFE...

SHE HOLDS UP TWO FINGERS AND SAYS, 'I'LL HAVE **FIVE** COFFEES PLEASE'!

WHAT POTATO CAN BE FOUND IN THE ROMAN COLOSSEUM?

GLADIATOR-**TATER!**

WHAT'S THE WORST THING THAT CAN HAPPEN TO A GEOGRAPHY TEACHER?

GETTING LOST!

WHY DID THE PHARAOH VISIT THE DENTIST?

BECAUSE **EGYPT** HIS TOOTH!

HISTORY & GEOGRAPHY

WHY WAS THE PERIOD BETWEEN 500 AD AND 900 AD KNOWN AS THE DARK AGES?

BECAUSE THOSE WERE THE DAYS OF THE **KNIGHTS**!

WHERE ARE KINGS AND QUEENS CROWNED?

ON THE **HEAD**!

WHAT TRAVELS AROUND THE WORLD BUT STAYS IN THE CORNER?

A **STAMP**!

WHAT DO YOU CALL DOGS WHO DIG UP ANCIENT ARTEFACTS?

BARKAEOLOGISTS!

HOW DID THE VIKINGS SEND SECRET MESSAGES?

NORSE CODE!

WHY IS THE PHARAOH ALWAYS BOASTING?

HE **SPHINX** HE'S THE BEST!

WHY WAS THE ARCHAEOLOGIST SAD?

HIS CAREER WAS IN **RUINS**!

HOW ARE FEET LIKE ANCIENT STORIES?

THEY'RE **LEG**-ENDS!

HISTORY & GEOGRAPHY

WHO INVENTED KING ARTHUR'S ROUND TABLE?

SIR CUMFERENCE!

WHAT'S THE BEST THING ABOUT SWITZERLAND?

I DON'T KNOW BUT THE FLAG'S A BIG **PLUS**!

WHERE DO PENS COME FROM?

PENNSYLVANIA!

WHAT'S BIG, WHITE, FURRY AND ALWAYS POINTS NORTH?

A POLAR **BEAR**ING!

HISTORY & GEOGRAPHY

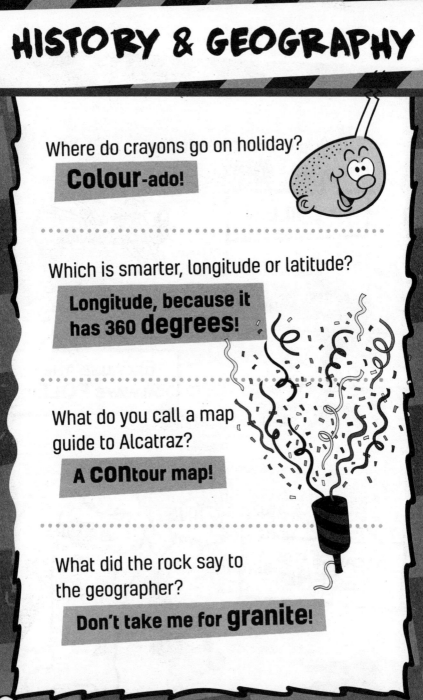

Where do crayons go on holiday?

Colour-ado!

Which is smarter, longitude or latitude?

Longitude, because it has 360 degrees!

What do you call a map guide to Alcatraz?

A CONtour map!

What did the rock say to the geographer?

Don't take me for granite!

Mountains aren't just funny...

They're hill-areas!

How do mountains see?

They peak!

What did the sea say to the shore?

Nothing, it just waved!

What rock group has four men that don't sing?

Mount Rushmore!

POP!

HI

HISTORY & GEOGRAPHY

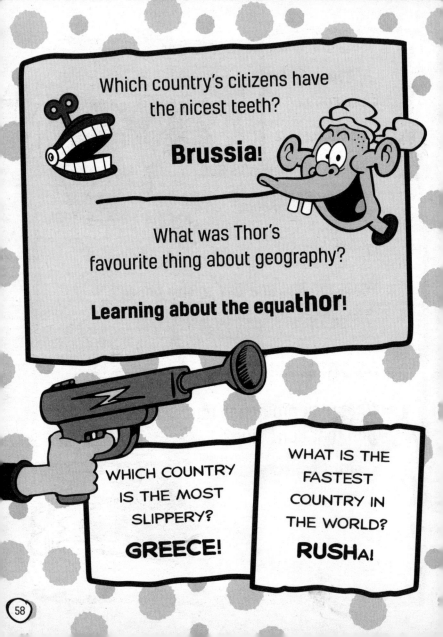

Which country's citizens have the nicest teeth?

Brussia!

What was Thor's favourite thing about geography?

Learning about the equaThor!

WHICH COUNTRY IS THE MOST SLIPPERY?

GREECE!

WHAT IS THE FASTEST COUNTRY IN THE WORLD?

RUSHA!

WHAT'S THE COLDEST COUNTRY?

CHILE!

What do you call a country populated entirely by donkeys?

An assaSSination!

Why didn't the hipster swim in the river?

It was too mainstream!

P.E.

WHAT DO YOU CALL A
SMALL POLE THAT CAN SWIM?

A TAD**POLE**!

★ ★ ★

WHAT STROKE DO SHEEP LIKE MOST?

THE **BAAAAA**CKSTROKE!

★ ★ ★

A FISH SWIMS INTO A WALL.

DAM!

HOW MUCH DOES IT COST
TO SWIM WITH SHARKS?

AN ARM AND A LEG!

★ ★ ★

WHAT DO YOU CALL A GOAT
THAT CAN SWIM REALLY FAST?

A MOTOR GOAT!

★ ★ ★

WHY SHOULD YOU NEVER
SWIM ON A FULL STOMACH?

**BECAUSE IT'S
EASIER TO SWIM
ON WATER!**

Someone asked for a donation towards the local swimming pool.

So I gave them a glass of water!

Why are spiders so good at swimming?

Because they have webbed feet!

Last night I dreamt I was swimming in orange soda.

It was just a Fanta-sea!

What does a search engine wear in the water?

Swimming Googles!

Which way round the pool do chickens swim?

Cluckwise!

Where do mummies swim?

In the **Dead** Sea!

Why do sharks only swim in salt water?

Because **pepper** water would make them sneeze!

WHAT KIND OF RACE IS NEVER RUN?

A **SWIMMING** RACE!

IS THIS POOL SAFE FOR DIVING?

IT **DEEP**ENDS!

DANGER!

WHY DID THE ELEPHANTS GET KICKED OUT OF THE SWIMMING POOL?

BECAUSE THEY COULDN'T KEEP THEIR **TRUNKS** UP!

WHY WAS THE MOUSE AFRAID OF SWIMMING?

CATFISH!

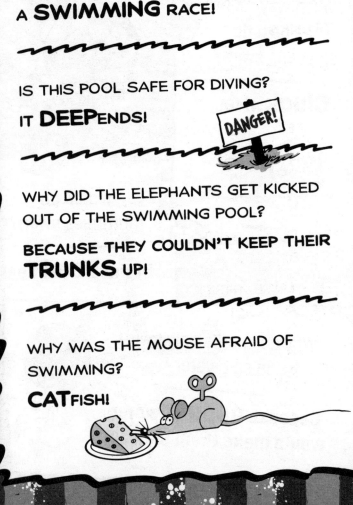

WHAT DO ELEPHANTS WEAR
TO GO SWIMMING?

TRUNKS!

I DIDN'T DO WELL IN MY
FOOTBALL TEAMWORK EXAM...

I DIDN'T **PASS!**

WHY DON'T BANKERS
RIDE BIKES?

THEY LOSE THEIR
BALANCE!

P.E.

WHAT LIGHTS UP A FOOTBALL PITCH AT NIGHT?

A FOOTBALL **MATCH**!

WHAT DOES A SNOWMAN USE TO GET AROUND?

AN **ICICLE**!

HOW DID THE HAIRDRESSER WIN THE BIKE RACE?

BY TAKING A SHORT **CUT**!

WHY DO FOOTBALLERS STRUGGLE TO EAT SANDWICHES?

THEY THINK THEY CAN'T USE THEIR HANDS!

P.E.

When is a bike not a bike?

When it turns into a driveway!

What's the best kind of bike?

A wheely good one!

What kind of bike likes camping and hill walks?

A mountain bike!

What happened when the bike fell in the river?

It was up the creek without a peddle!

JOKE BOX

Why was the bike maker so rubbish?

He just couldn't get a handle on it!

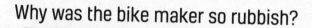

When is a football pitch like a triangle?

When somebody takes a corner!

What's a bike's favourite type of moustache?

A handlebar!

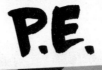

P.E.

WHAT DO YOU CALL
SOMEONE WHO SELLS BIKES
DOOR TO DOOR?

A **PEDDLAR**!

★ ★ ★

WHY DID THE BIKE HAVE TO REST?

IT WAS **TWO TYRED**!

★ ★ ★

HOW DO BIKES HELP THE ENVIRONMENT?

BY **RECYCLING**!

★ ★ ★

WHAT HAPPENS WHEN A BIKE
GETS DISTRACTED?

IT GOES OFF ON A **TANDEM**!

WHAT DO YOU GET IF YOU
CROSS A BIKE AND A FLOWER?

BICYCLE **PETALS**!

★ ★ ★

WHAT'S THE HARDEST THING
ABOUT LEARNING TO RIDE A BIKE?

THE **GROUND**!

★ ★ ★

WHY WAS THE FOOTBALLER COVERED IN SPIT?

SHE WAS ALWAYS **DRIBBLING**!

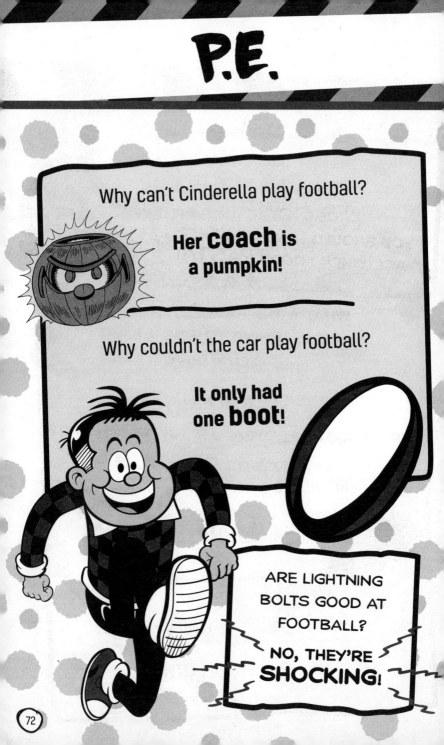

Why can't Cinderella play football?

Her coach is a pumpkin!

Why couldn't the car play football?

It only had one boot!

ARE LIGHTNING BOLTS GOOD AT FOOTBALL?

NO, THEY'RE **SHOCKING!**

MY SISTER TOLD ME I COULDN'T MAKE A BICYCLE OUT OF SPAGHETTI.

YOU SHOULD HAVE SEEN HER FACE WHEN I RODE **PASTA**!

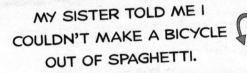

How do footballers stay cool?

They sit next to their fans!

What does a cyclist ride in winter?

An icicle!

How did the barber win the bike race?

He took a short cut!

P.E.

Why did the square and triangle go to the gym?

To stay in **shape**!

Why did the boy take his bike to bed with him?

Because he didn't want to sleep walk!

Those new rugby matches in space will never take off.

There's just no atmosphere!

74

What does a turtle need to ride a bike?

A shellmet!

I'm trying to learn rugby but can't quite get it right.

Every time I think I've scored, the coach says, 'Good try!'

What insect lives in your floor and is good at scoring tries?

The rugbee!

Once you've seen one rugby joke...

You've seen a maul!

P.E.

WHERE DO TENNIS PLAYERS GO TO DANCE?

A TENNIS **BALL**!

WHAT DID ONE TENNIS BALL SAY TO THE OTHER TENNIS BALL?

SEE YOU A**ROUND**!

IN TENNIS, WHAT DO YOU SERVE BUT NEVER EAT?

A TENNIS **BALL**!

THEY'VE INVENTED A NEW VERSION OF RUGBY WHERE ONLY PEOPLE WHO WEAR GLASSES CAN PLAY IT...

IT'S A NON-**CONTACT** SPORT!

WHAT TIME DO TENNIS PLAYERS GO TO BED?

TENNISH!

WHAT DO YOU CALL A GIRL STANDING IN THE MIDDLE OF A TENNIS COURT?

AN**NET**TE!

FOOD & DRINK

What do ghosts like to have with their apple pie?

I scream!

What do you get if you cross a snake with a pie?

A piethon!

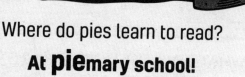

Where do pies learn to read?

At piemary school!

Who makes the best apple pies?

Granny Smith!

What does a pie say
after a huge meal?

That was filling!

What do you get if you eat
too much pumpkin pie?

Au**tumn-y** **ache!**

Why did the apple pie cry?

Somebody hurt its **peelings!**

FOOD & DRINK

HOW DOES A BAKER KEEP TRACK OF HOW MANY PIES THEY'VE MADE?

A **PIE** CHART!

WHAT WAS THE GHOST'S FAVOURITE PUDDING?

BOOBERRY MUFFINS!

I HAD A SHEPHERD'S PIE FOR LUNCH TODAY.

THEY WEREN'T HAPPY ABOUT IT!

WHAT'S A MATHEMATICIAN'S FAVOURITE TYPE OF PIE?

3.14159265359...

WHY ARE MUSHROOMS INVITED TO PARTIES?

BECAUSE THEY'RE SUCH **FUNGIS!**

WHY DID THE PIE GO TO THE DENTIST?

IT NEEDED A **FILLING!**

WHAT DO YOU CALL A POTATO WITH RIGHT ANGLES?

A SQUARE **ROOT**!

WHAT VEGETABLE LOVES POGO STICKS?

A **SPRING** ONION!

EXTRA LARDY CRISPS

FOOD & DRINK

WHAT DAY OF THE WEEK DO POTATOES HATE MOST?

FRYDAY!

WHAT DO YOU SAY TO A LOUD VEGETABLE?

TURNIP DOWN!

WHAT WAS THE SNOWMAN DOING IN THE VEGETABLE PATCH?

PICKING HIS NOSE!

WHY DO FUNGI HAVE TO PAY DOUBLE BUS FARES?

BECAUSE THEY TAKE UP TOO **MUSHROOM**!

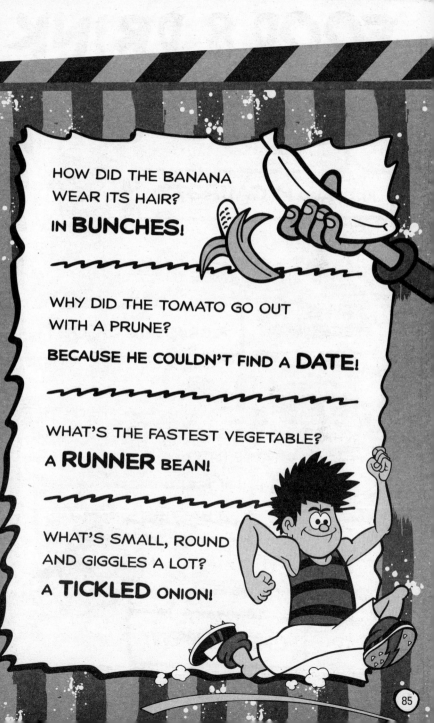

HOW DID THE BANANA
WEAR ITS HAIR?

IN **BUNCHES**!

WHY DID THE TOMATO GO OUT
WITH A PRUNE?

BECAUSE HE COULDN'T FIND A DATE!

WHAT'S THE FASTEST VEGETABLE?

A **RUNNER** BEAN!

WHAT'S SMALL, ROUND
AND GIGGLES A LOT?

A **TICKLED** ONION!

FOOD & DRINK

HOW DO YOU TURN SOUP INTO GOLD?

JUST ADD **14 CARROTS**!

WHAT'S GREEN AND GOES TO A SUMMER CAMP?

A BRUSSELS **SCOUT**!

WHAT DO YOU CALL A SHEEP THAT WORKS IN A FISH AND CHIP SHOP?

A BATTERING **RAM**!

HOW DOES A TRAIN EAT?

CHEW CHEW!

FOOD & DRINK

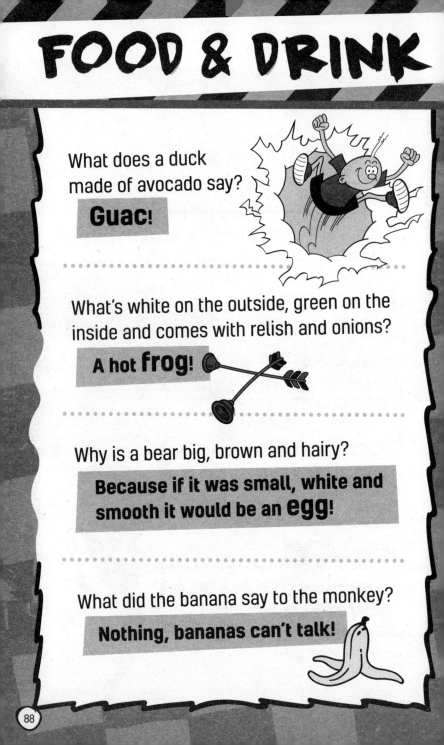

What does a duck made of avocado say?

Guac!

What's white on the outside, green on the inside and comes with relish and onions?

A hot frog!

Why is a bear big, brown and hairy?

Because if it was small, white and smooth it would be an egg!

What did the banana say to the monkey?

Nothing, bananas can't talk!

A friend told me that all apples are yellow.

I told him, 'That's bananas!'

What do you give a sausage dog with a fever?

Mustard – it's the best thing for a hot dog!

When does bread rise?

When you yeast expect it!

FOOD & DRINK

HOW MUCH FOOD DOES
A CAT HAVE AT BREAKFAST?

A **MEOW**THFUL!

★ ★ ★

DID YOU HEAR THE RUMOUR ABOUT BUTTER?

WELL, I'M NOT GOING TO **SPREAD** IT!

★ ★ ★

WHERE DO YOU LEARN TO MAKE ICE CREAM?

AT **SUNDAE** SCHOOL!

HOW MANY APPLES GROW
ON A TREE?

ALL OF THEM!

★ ★ ★

WHY DID THE BANANA GO TO THE HOSPITAL?

IT WASN'T **PEELING** WELL!

★ ★ ★

WHAT HAPPENS WHEN AN EGG HEARS A JOKE?

IT **CRACKS** UP!

FOOD & DRINK

What do you get if you cross a cheetah with a burger?

Fast food!

WHICH CHEESE
IS MADE
BACKWARDS?
EDAM!

WHAT DO YOU CALL CHEESE THAT DOESN'T BELONG TO YOU?

NACHO CHEESE!

What do cats have for breakfast?

Mice Krispies!

What do you call a man with gravy and potatoes on his head?

Stew!

Why did the girl sprinkle sugar on her pillows?

She wanted to have SWeet dreams!

Did you hear what happened to the snail when he was stood on?

He was really crushed!

What do you call a snail who sails the seven seas?

A snailor!

Why wasn't the giraffe paying attention?

She had her head in the clouds!

Why do giraffes have long necks?

Because their feet smell!

I just learned how to speak parrot!

I just learned how to speak parrot!

How do slugs send post?

By snail mail!

ANIMALS

WHAT'S A PARROT'S FAVOURITE GAME?

HIDE AND **SPEAK**!

HOW DO YOU MAKE A BABY SNAKE CRY?

TAKE AWAY ITS **RATTLE**!

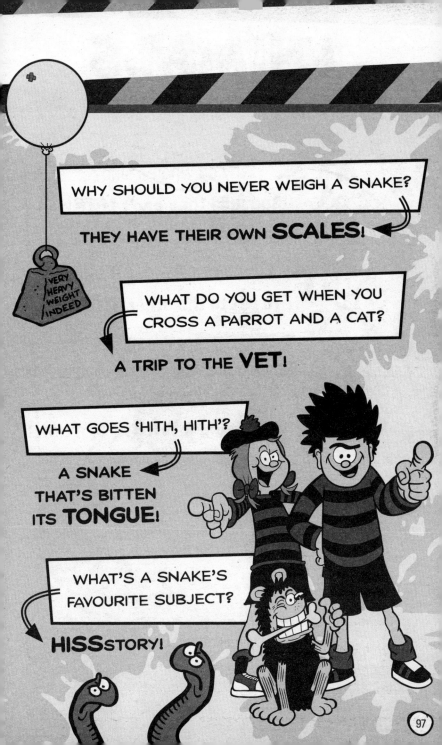

WHY SHOULD YOU NEVER WEIGH A SNAKE?

THEY HAVE THEIR OWN **SCALES**!

VERY
HEAVY
WEIGHT
INDEED

WHAT DO YOU GET WHEN YOU CROSS A PARROT AND A CAT?

A TRIP TO THE **VET**!

WHAT GOES 'HITH, HITH'?

A SNAKE THAT'S BITTEN ITS **TONGUE**!

WHAT'S A SNAKE'S FAVOURITE SUBJECT?

HISSSTORY!

ANIMALS

Why do whales sing?
Because they can't talk!

Why did the whale cross the ocean?
To get to the other side!

Why did the whale want to stay
at the party?

She was having a whale of a time!

Why was the whale sad?

Because it was a blue whale!

How do whales make decisions?

They flipper coin!

How did the octopus make the whale laugh?

With tentickles!

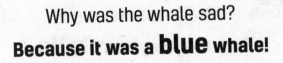

ANIMALS

WHERE DOES A RABBIT GO WHEN IT FEELS SICK?

THE **HOP**SPITAL!

WHY WAS THE BUNNY SO ANNOYING?

HE KEPT **RABBITING** ON!

WHAT DO YOU CALL A MAN WITH A RABBIT LIVING IN HIS JUMPER?

WARREN!

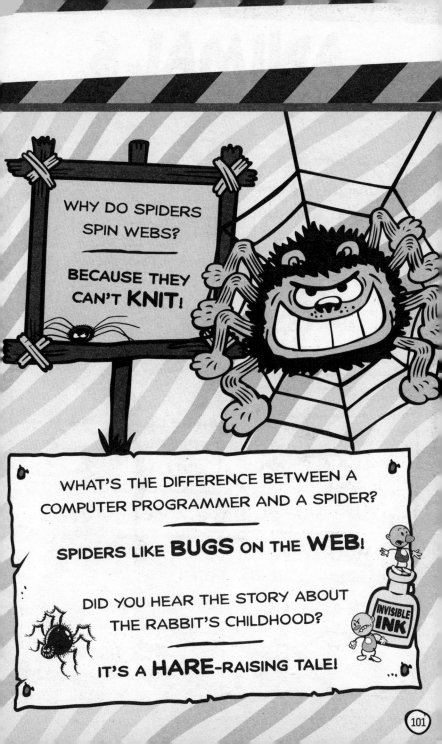

WHY DO SPIDERS SPIN WEBS?

BECAUSE THEY CAN'T **KNIT**!

WHAT'S THE DIFFERENCE BETWEEN A COMPUTER PROGRAMMER AND A SPIDER?

SPIDERS LIKE **BUGS** ON THE **WEB**!

DID YOU HEAR THE STORY ABOUT THE RABBIT'S CHILDHOOD?

IT'S A **HARE**-RAISING TALE!

INVISIBLE **INK**

ANIMALS

WHERE DO SPIDERS HANG OUT?

ON THE **WEB**!

WHAT'S A SPIDER'S FAVOURITE HOBBY?

FLY FISHING!

WHAT'S THE BEST JOB FOR A SPIDER?

A **WEB** DESIGNER!

WHY DID THE SPIDER BUY A CAR?

HE WANTED TO GO FOR A **SPIN**!

WHAT DO SPIDERS EAT IN PARIS?

FRENCH **FLIES**!

HOW TALL ARE SPIDERS?

EIGHT FEET!

ANIMALS

What kind of monkey is the best to hang out with?

A funkey!

What kind of monkey can fly?

A hot air baboon!

WHAT DO YOU CALL AN EXPLODING MONKEY?

A BaBOOM!

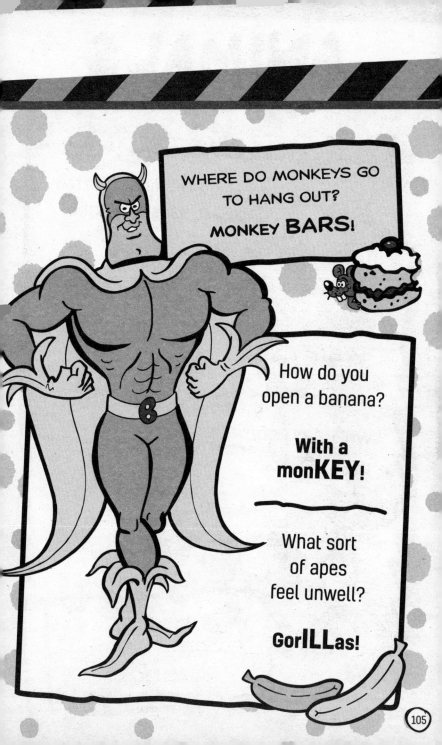

WHERE DO MONKEYS GO TO HANG OUT?

MONKEY **BARS!**

How do you open a banana?

With a monKEY!

What sort of apes feel unwell?

GorILLas!

HOW DOES A WASP
GET AROUND TOWN?

IT RIDES ON THE **BUZZ**!

WHAT SPORT DO WASPS PLAY?

STING PONG!

WHERE DO SQUIRRELS WATCH TV?

ON **NUT**FLIX!

WHAT'S A SQUIRREL'S FAVOURITE BALLET?

THE **NUTCRACKER!**

WHAT DID THE TREE SAY TO THE SQUIRREL?

LEAF ME ALONE!

I'D MAKE FUN OF WHAT SQUIRRELS EAT...

BUT IT'D BE **ACORN**Y JOKE!

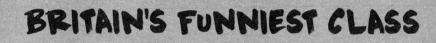

BRITAIN'S FUNNIEST CLASS

After much consideration from the judges,
the shortlisted jokes for Beano
Britain's Funniest Class 2021 are...

WHERE'S THE BEST PLACE TO
TAKE A DOG FOR A WALK?

LEEDS!

ST JOHN THE BAPTIST PRIMARY SCHOOL, LEICESTER

KNOCK-KNOCK!

WHO'S THERE?

JUSTIN.

JUSTIN WHO?

JUSTIN **TIME** TO READ BEANO!

UPTON MEADOWS PRIMARY, NORTHAMPTON

WHAT DID THE TEACHER SAY TO THE
COMIC LOVER AS A PUNISHMENT?

THERE WILL **BEANO** COMICS FOR YOU!

GREYSTONES PRIMARY SCHOOL, SHEFFIELD

WHY DID THE MOBILE PHONE GO FOR AN EYE TEST?

BECAUSE IT LOST ITS CONTACTS!

HAMPTON HILL JUNIOR SCHOOL, HAMPTON HILL

WHAT DID THE FACEMASK SAY TO THE MOUTH?

LET ME COVER FOR YOU!

FORTHILL PRIMARY SCHOOL, DUNDEE

WHAT DID THE SCARY PANDA SAY?

BAM-BOOOOO!

UFFCULME PRIMARY SCHOOL, CULLOMPTON

WHAT'S THE COLDEST CHRISTMAS FOOD?

PIGS IN BLANKETS!

FINTON HOUSE SCHOOL, LONDON

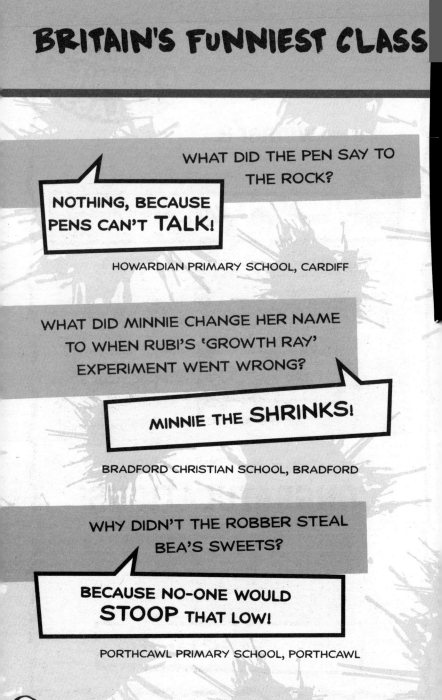

WHAT DID THE PEN SAY TO THE ROCK?

NOTHING, BECAUSE PENS CAN'T **TALK!**

HOWARDIAN PRIMARY SCHOOL, CARDIFF

WHAT DID MINNIE CHANGE HER NAME TO WHEN RUBI'S 'GROWTH RAY' EXPERIMENT WENT WRONG?

MINNIE THE **SHRINKS!**

BRADFORD CHRISTIAN SCHOOL, BRADFORD

WHY DIDN'T THE ROBBER STEAL BEA'S SWEETS?

BECAUSE NO-ONE WOULD **STOOP** THAT LOW!

PORTHCAWL PRIMARY SCHOOL, PORTHCAWL

And the **winner** is...

FORTHILL PRIMARY SCHOOL, DUNDEE

CONGRATULATIONS!

WHAT DID THE FACEMASK
SAY TO THE MOUTH?

LET ME **COVER** FOR YOU!